Boost Serialization within C++
Advanced Data Persistence

Table of Contents

Chapter 1. Introduction

Welcome to this Special Report - a deep dive into the well-established and powerful tool within the C library, 'Boost Serialization.' This comprehensive report will provide you with insights into advanced data persistence techniques in C, a highly technical topic that forms a crucial cornerstone in large scale software development projects. Presented in a down-to-earth manner, it aims to unravel the complexities of Boost Serialization through practical examples and clear illustrations, transforming the task from daunting to doable. Whether you are a seasoned developer or a novice, this report has something to offer, and we'll leave no stone unturned to ensure you understand, implement, and master the Boost Serialization in C++. Let's embark on this journey of intricacies and complexities, with the assurance that by the end, you'll gain admirable knowledge and versatile skills.

Chapter 2. Understanding Boost and Its Importance in C++

Boost is a remarkable set of libraries for C++, furnishing numerous pragmatic and versatile ways to extend the core language. From smart pointers to lambda expressions and serialization libraries, Boost is essential in achieving productive, efficient, and robust software applications.

One of the libraries residing within the Boost family is Boost.Serialization, a powerful tool that enables C++ programmers to persist and restore applications' state into and from storage media. Depending on the nature and requirement of the applications, the storage medium can range from text files, binary files, archives to network sockets, and other devices that support I/O operations.

2.1. Why Use Boost?

The Boost library is an aggregation of individually developed and maintained libraries, ranging from foundational components like smart pointers to specialized libraries like the Quaternion and Octonion class templates. Boost, therefore, is not only a library but a vast ecosystem that fulfills a plethora of programming needs.

Choosing Boost for a project can boost productivity, reduce development time, ensure code portability and do so much more for a developer.

- **Efficiency**: Boost libraries are designed and developed by experienced C++ programmers, ensuring best practices and optimal usage of the language features. This results in highly efficient and performant code.

- **Portability**: Designed to be portable, the Boost library ensures developers can write code once and use it across different platforms and compilers. It is adaptable for most modern operating systems, including many versions of Windows and UNIX.

- **Extensibility**: Boost libraries are extensible and can be combined to build more complex application features. They have also been designed to accommodate easy customization, resulting in a highly adaptable codebase.

- **Standardization**: Many libraries in Boost eventually find their way into C standard libraries. Using Boost not only ensures code quality and efficiency but also secures code's future compatibility with the C Standard.

2.2. Spotlight on Boost.Serialization

The Boost.Serialization library provides a uniform and flexible framework for serializing C++ objects. The library's main role is to make it easier to save the state of a program in a storage medium and to restore it whenever needed.

This library can be customized to any requirements, and it takes care of the most tedious and error-prone parts of serialization. It supports most of the C++ data types and many user-defined types, managing both the saving and the loading phase.

2.3. What is Boost.Serialization Useful For?

Data Serialization has a critical role in the field of software development. It can be used in numerous ways:

- **Persistence**: Store the current state of your application and restore it later. This is essential for applications that need to maintain their state even after shutdown, such as games or editing tools.

- **Deep Copying**: Make deep copies of complex data structures. With Boost.Serialization, it becomes considerably easier, as it's able to follow pointers and manage copies of pointed data.

- **IPC (Inter-Process Communication)**: Serialize objects to send over a network, enabling two applications to talk and share objects with each other.

- **Undo/Redo systems**: By saving the application state after each operation, the user can later undo or redo the last operations.

2.4. Boost.Serialization Features

Boost.Serialization comes with several key features that enhance its usability and functionality:

- **Versioning**: The library supports versioning for class templates, enabling backward compatibility with older versions of serialized classes.

- **Portability**: Boost.Serialization ensures portability across different platforms and compilers. Serialized archives created on one platform can be reliably de-serialized on another.

- **Error-handling**: It provides a robust and reliable error detection and exception-handling mechanism.

- **Automatic serialization**: For most cases, serialization code for C++ classes and containers can be automatically generated, ensuring you spend less time writing boilerplate code.

Approaching Boost, and particularly Boost.Serialization, can initially feel challenging. However, understanding its importance and the value it can bring to software projects is step one in mastering it. Following chapters will delve into the technical details of using Boost.Serialization, providing practical examples and clear guidelines to transform this daunting task into a doable one.

Chapter 3. Introduction to Data Persistence: Basics and Theories

In any advanced computing operation or process, as we move from a basic single-use application towards a complex software environment, there surfaces a requirement of a broader procedure - the persistence of data. Data persistence can be simply understood as the ability of data to outlast the application process that created it. For developers working with C++, Boost Serialization library is a powerful resource for data persistence. Before diving deep into the complexities of this library, let's unpack the basic concepts and theories of data persistence.

3.1. Understanding Data Persistence

Data persistence is fundamentally about retaining data structures between different runs of a program or even among different program instances. This notion serves as the basic premise for various computing phenomena, including web cookies, session data, and indeed large databases.

Typically, program data ceases to exist once the application's process is terminated — it's transient. However, to extend the life of this data beyond the life cycle of an application, it needs to be persisted. Data persistence does this job—it saves the state of data into a durable medium such as disk storage or a database, and later retrieves it when necessary. This enables data to survive various events such as application crashes, system failures, or planned system reboots.

But, how can we take care of complex data types, like composite data structures and objects? Serialization comes to the rescue right there, serving as a bridge in the data persistence process.

3.2. Serialization: The Link to Data Persistence

Serialization is a process during which an object's state is converted into a format that can be persisted or transported. The purpose of serialization is to allow data structures or objects to be saved on a disk or sent over a network.

Imagine your application involves a complex data structure, say, a tree or a graph—not just simple integers or strings. Now, our disk or database doesn't understand a bisecting node, a unique edge or a leaf node. It just understands bytes. Here comes the role of serialization—it transforms a complex object or a data structure into a contiguous sequence of bytes. In the reverse process, deserialization, we convert this byte stream back into the original object.

3.3. C++ Perspective on Serialization

In a multi-paradigm language like C, data takes multiple forms—primitives, objects, containers or something more complex. The C Standard Library does not include a built-in mechanism for serialization, unlike some other languages. Hence, for any C++ application that requires data persistence, a third-party library like Boost Serialization comes into play.

3.4. Enter, Boost Serialization

The Boost Libraries are a widely used, extensive collection of open-source C libraries that significantly expand the set of available libraries, compared to the Standard Library. Among them, the Boost Serialization library is a high-quality solution to serialize and persist virtually any data type in C.

Its capabilities are not just limited to primitive data types or STL containers, classes, and structures. They climb up the ladder of complexity to manage pointers, references, and class hierarchies, too. For instance, reference tracking ensures that an object is only serialized once and that references before and after serialization point to the same object.

Another critical feature of Boost Serialization is its compatibility with diverse and customized archives types. An archive refers to a medium where you save (serialize) your object. Data can be stored in text, binary, or XML format as per the requirements.

3.5. Importance of Using Boost Serialization

In an industry where data is the new gold, efficient and reliable data persistence mechanisms are vital for seizing competitive advantage. For a C++ software application, the Boost serialization library offers a highly flexible and portable mechanism for persistent data storage and retrieval.

Imagine a gaming application. Would you want your user to start from scratch every time they open the application? Definitely not. Here, you will need data persistence to save and retrieve game statuses.

Data persistence aided by serialization can also be critical for application safety. For instance, an airline system holds flight details, including vital data like flight schedules, passenger details, and emergency contacts. Any crash resulting in data loss could lead to catastrophic consequences. It is here that data persistence plays its part, ensuring system reliability and data safety.

3.6. Concluding Remarks

From a broader lens, serialization and data persistence play a cardinal role in making software reliable, secure, and user-friendly. As we move toward larger, more complex applications, understanding and correctly using Boost Serialization library becomes a fundamental skill for a C++ developer. It opens the doors for efficient saving and retrieving of complex data, making sure our applications are ready to survive the test of system crash or shutdown while maintaining the desired user experience.

In the next chapters, we will dive deeper into the practical aspects of the Boost Serialization library, starting with setting up the environment, coding serialization for simple and complex data types, and using Boost archives. We will also provide troubleshooting guidance and best practice advice. By the end of this journey, you will have mastered the art and science of serialization and data persistence in C++. Stay tuned!

Chapter 4. Diving into Boost Serialization: Concepts and Principles

The world of C++ provides a multitude of libraries that aid developers in writing effective and efficient code. One of these is the Boost library, which offers a wide array of utilities, yet today we'll zoom in on one of its most potent tools: Boost Serialization.

Boost Serialization facilitates saving and restoring the state of C++ objects in a portable and easy-to-use manner. Data persistence is a cornerstone, a heavyweight enterprise that lies at the very heart of data-focused applications. Let's pull back the curtain on its core concepts and principles.

4.1. What is Serialization?

Before we delve deeper into Boost Serialization, it's vital to understand the basic concept of serialization itself. In essence, serialization is a process that transforms an object's state into a format suitable for storage or transmission. This format can be a file, a database, memory, or a network connection.

Consider a practical example. Suppose you are developing a game and want to store game state at specific checkpoints. You would need to 'serialize' the state of all the entities in the game such as player stats, enemy positions, or items collected. Conversely, to restore a game state, you 'deserialize' the saved state back into the game objects.

4.2. The Role of Boost Serialization

Boost Serialization is a versatile tool that enables you to serialize and deserialize C++ objects in a clean, versatile, and efficient manner. It is designed to be easy to use, regardless of the complexity of your objects. It can handle intricate relationships between objects, including polymorphic types, objects containing pointers, and recursive data structures.

Boost Serialization's design philosophy centers around three key principles: Ease of Use, Transparency, and Portability. The library achieves this by seamlessly integrating with C++, preserving a highly familiar programming style, and supporting a range of serialization formats.

4.3. Understanding the Working of Boost Serialization

A typical serialization process with Boost involves an object and a stream. The object is what you want to serialize, and the stream represents where the serialized data is to be stored or sent - it could be a disk file, stringstream, or across a network.

Serialize and deserialize your objects using Boost Serialization's stream operators << and >> respectively. Boost Serialization automatically ensures data is sent in a correct and efficient order, making it almost effortless to serialize complex data structures.

To illustrate, take a look at this simplistic example:

```
#include <boost/archive/text_oarchive.hpp>
#include <boost/archive/text_iarchive.hpp>

struct Data {
```

```
    int x, y;

    template<class Archive>
    void serialize(Archive& ar, const unsigned int
version) {
        ar & x;
        ar & y;
    }
};

// ...
Data d1 = {1, 2}, d2;

// serialization
{
    boost::archive::text_oarchive oa(std::cout);
    oa << d1;
}

// deserialization
{
    boost::archive::text_iarchive ia(std::cin);
    ia >> d2;
}
```

In the code above, we've defined a struct Data with two members x
and y, and then serialized and deserialized it using Boost
Serialization.

4.4. Serialization Techniques

There are three primary methods for serializing an object using
Boost Serialization:

1. Member function

2. Friend function

3. Free standing function

The first approach involves declaring a member function `serialize` in the object's class. This function should be a template function, accepting any type of archive. The function doesn't need to be public. You can make it private or protected and boost::serialization::access can still call it.

The friend and free-standing function approaches are used when for whatever reason, it's not advisable or possible to modify the class you want to serialize.

4.5. Handing Versioning of Classes

Software usually evolves over time, and so do the data structures used. Boost Serialization provides a system to manage changes in class definitions over time, through versioning. This helps maintain backward compatibility with older serialized instances of the class.

To use versioning, include a `version` parameter in your `serialize` function, and conditionally process data based on this value. You'll also need to use the `BOOST_CLASS_VERSION` macro to associate a version number with your class.

Whatever reasons brought you to Boost Serialization, the journey to mastering it involves embracing its core principles and getting your hands dirty with code. Becoming familiar and proficient with this C++ boost library opens up critical avenues of data persistence, making you a much more flexible and versatile developer, leagues beyond ordinary scope. So keep diving, keep exploring - the depth and breadth of Boost Serialization await.

Chapter 5. Boost Serialization and Its Application in Data Persistence

Boost Serialization is a comprehensive library in C++ designed for saving intricate in-memory data structures, known as serialization, and reviving them, known as deserialization. By maintaining the relationships between objects, it serves as a crucial tool for a range of applications such as writing and reading binary files, maintaining program states, object persistence, and more.

5.1. Understanding Serialization in Boost

At its core, serialization is the process of transforming complex data structures into a stream of bytes, which can then be saved to disk, sent over the network or loaded into memory. Boost Serialization is designed to handle the serialization of C++ data types and user-defined classes flawly. Notably, it supports:

- C++ fundamental types (char, int, float, etc.)

- C++ STL containers (std::vector, std::set, std::map, etc.)

- User-defined types (classes and structs)

The key functions involved in the serialization process are:

- `void serialize(Archive &ar, const unsigned int version)`: applicable for both serialization and deserialization. Here, Archive can be any type, such as binary_i/oarchive, text_i/oarchive, etc., depending on your specific needs.

- `template<class Archive> void save(Archive & ar, const unsigned` int version) const: specifically for serialization.

- template<class Archive> void load(Archive & ar, const unsigned int version): specifically for deserialization.

To differentiate between the save and load processes in the serialize function, one can utilize the Archive::is_saving or Archive::is_loading methods.

5.2. Applying Boost Serialization

Let's delve into the intricacies and practicalities of Boost Serialization with a basic example:

```
#include <boost/archive/text_oarchive.hpp>
#include <boost/archive/text_iarchive.hpp>

class student {
    // either friend your access method
    friend class boost::serialization::access;

    template<class Archive> void serialize(Archive & ar,
const unsigned int version){
        ar & ID;
        ar & name;
    }

    int ID;
    std::string name;
public:
    student(){}
    student(int id, std::string n) : ID(id), name(n) {}
};

void save() {
    // make an instance of student
```

```
    student s(10, "John Doe");

    // create and open a character archive for output
    std::ofstream ofs("student.txt");

    // save data to archive
    boost::archive::text_oarchive oa(ofs);
    oa << s;
}

void load() {
    // construct a new instance
    student new_s;

    // create and open an archive for input
    std::ifstream ifs("student.txt");
    boost::archive::text_iarchive ia(ifs);

    // load data from archive into new_s
    ia >> new_s;
}
```

Here, our student class has two attributes - ID and name. The serialize
function, which contains these two attributes, are written to a file on
serialization and read back into a fresh instance of student during
deserialization.

5.3. Delving into the Split Member Function

In the above example, serialization and deserialization are handled
together by one function void serialize(Archive &ar). However,
Boost also provides the mechanism to split them into two different
functions: save and load. It can be useful when one has complex,

conditional logic that depends on if objects are being saved or loaded.

Here is a similar example using the split member function:

```cpp
#include <boost/archive/text_oarchive.hpp>
#include <boost/archive/text_iarchive.hpp>
#include <boost/serialization/split_member.hpp>

class student {
    friend class boost::serialization::access;

    template<class Archive> void save(Archive & ar,
const unsigned int version) const {
        ar << ID;
        ar << name;
    }

    template<class Archive> void load(Archive & ar,
const unsigned int version) {
        ar >> ID;
        ar >> name;
    }

    BOOST_SERIALIZATION_SPLIT_MEMBER()

    int ID;
    std::string name;
public:
    student(){}
    student(int id, std::string n) : ID(id), name(n) {}
};

// save and load functions remain same as before
```

In this revised code, we have placed function

BOOST_SERIALIZATION_SPLIT_MEMBER() in the student class to separate the save and load processes, which are explicitly handled in the provided methods.

5.4. Serialization of Container Classes

Boost Serialization also supports container classes. Here is an example:

```
#include <boost/archive/text_oarchive.hpp>
#include <boost/archive/text_iarchive.hpp>
#include <vector>

class student {
    friend class boost::serialization::access;

    template<class Archive> void serialize(Archive & ar,
const unsigned int version){
        ar & ID;
        ar & name;
    }

    int ID;
    std::string name;
public:
    student(){}
    student(int id, std::string n) : ID(id), name(n) {}
};

void save() {
    // make a vector of student
    std::vector<student> s;
    s.push_back(student(10, "John Doe"));
```

```cpp
        s.push_back(student(12, "Jane Doe"));

        // create and open a character archive for output
        std::ofstream ofs("students.txt");

        // save data to archive
        boost::archive::text_oarchive oa(ofs);
        oa << s;
}

void load() {
        // construct a new instance
        std::vector<student> new_s;

        // create and open an archive for input
        std::ifstream ifs("students.txt");
        boost::archive::text_iarchive ia(ifs);

        // load data from archive into new_s
        ia >> new_s;
}
```

To summarize, Boost Serialization is a powerful mechanism for data persistence in C++, handling a variety of data structures and types. Whether it is serialized into text or binary, the flexibility of the Boost Serialization library is commendable. Understanding and implementing this library, thus, represents a valuable skill that can aid in efficient and smooth software development.

Chapter 6. Getting Hands-On: Coding Examples with Boost Serialization

Before diving headfirst into coding examples, let's initiate by refreshing the basic understanding of Boost.Serialization. Essentially, it is a library engineered for the task of serializing and deserializing data, meaning it converts data into a format that can be stored or transmitted and later be reconstructed.

6.1. An overview of Boost.Serialization

One of the strong suits of Boost.Serialization is its ability to seamlessly serialize a wide array of data types, including user-defined types, collections, and smart pointers. Conventional serialization may encompass writing object state into a store (such as a file) or transmitting it over a network to a distinct machine, then reading the object state from the store to generate a copy of the object.

Now, we'll transition to coding examples, showcasing the mechanism in a practical setting.

6.2. Setting up Boost

To kick things off, we'll need the Boost library set up in your development environment.

```
#include <boost/archive/text_oarchive.hpp>
#include <boost/archive/text_iarchive.hpp>
```

```
#include <boost/serialization/string.hpp>
#include <boost/serialization/vector.hpp>
#include <boost/serialization/map.hpp>
```

These include directives are enough for most applications as it encapsulates text archives for serializing data and the common collection classes.

6.3. Simple Serialization & Deserialization

We will initially craft a code piece representing a simple employee object. The {}, () and <> are placeholders where you'll need to substitute valid C++ code. This is a general approach in technical explanations.

```cpp
class Employee {
public:
    Employee() {}
    Employee(std::string const& name, int id) :
name_(name), id_(id) {}
    // Rest of your code goes here
private:
    friend class boost::serialization::access;

    template<class Archive>
    void serialize(Archive & ar, const unsigned int
version) {
        ar & name_;
        ar & id_;
    }

    std::string name_;
    int id_;
```

```
};
```

In the above code, {} is an identifier representing a default constructor while <boost::serialization::string> corresponds to a class template that facilitates serialization of strings. This code won't perform any operation but it forms the groundwork for future operations.

Let's serialize an instance of Employee.

```
Employee emp("John Doe", 123);
std::ofstream ofs("employee");
boost::archive::text_oarchive oa(ofs);
oa << emp;
ofs.close();
```

This operation's outcome is a file named 'employee' that contains 'John Doe' and '123'.

Now let's recover that Employee instance.

```
Employee newEmp;
std::ifstream ifs("employee");
boost::archive::text_iarchive ia(ifs);
ia >> newEmp;
ifs.close();
```

Post the execution of this code section, newEmp will contain the serialized data, i.e., 'John Doe' and '123'.

6.4. Serializing & Deserializing Collections

Serializing a collection is no different from serializing a single object.

```
std::vector<Employee> employees;

// Add employees to vector
employees.push_back(Employee("John Doe", 123));
employees.push_back(Employee("Jane Doe", 456));

std::ofstream ofs("employees.vec");
boost::archive::text_oarchive oa(ofs);
oa << employees;
ofs.close();
```

Deserializing these objects is just as straightforward.

```
std::vector<Employee> newEmployees;
std::ifstream ifs("employees.vec");
boost::archive::text_iarchive ia(ifs);
ia >> newEmployees;
ifs.close();
```

6.5. Serializing & Deserializing pointers

When it comes to serializing pointers, a little more effort is required. This is chiefly because the serialize() function should save or load the content the pointer is pointing to, not the pointer itself. The Boost.Serialization library provides utilities to diligently handle pointer serialization.

```cpp
class Base {
public:
    virtual ~Base() {}
    // Your code here
};

class Derived : public Base {
public:
    // Your code here
private:
    template<class Archive>
    void serialize(Archive & ar, const unsigned int
version) {
        ar &
boost::serialization::base_object<Base>(*this);
    }
};

Derived* p = new Derived;
std::ofstream ofs("pointer");
{
    boost::archive::text_oarchive oa(ofs);
    oa << p;
}
delete p;

Derived* pNew = nullptr;
std::ifstream ifs("pointer");
{
    boost::archive::text_iarchive ia(ifs);
    ia >> pNew;
}
```

```
delete pNew;
```

Boost.Serialization extends beyond the examples given. Its flexibility, power, and convenient syntax make it an essential tool for C++ developers. Exploit the knowledge you gained from this in-depth exploration to handle larger and more complex serialization tasks. Explore the other facets of Boost.Serialization, such as polymorphic archives, XML and binary archives, and non-default constructors.

As with any potent software tool, the potential to use the Boost.Serialization library effectively depends greatly on the care, ingenuity, and understanding brought forth by the user (you!). To this end, practice, experiment, and explore - your software will benefit greatly by doing so.

Chapter 7. Exploring Advanced Features of Boost Serialization

Boost Serialization is a succulent dish on the buffet of seasoned developers, particularly those embroiled in the web of C. This powerful tool within the C library helps in preserving data between separate invocations of a program, often a critical aspect of computing. To fully utilize Boost Serialization, we need to carefully dissect the nuances of its more advanced features. So let's dive right in without any further ado.

7.1. Understanding Object Serialization and Tracking

To begin with, object tracking is a crucial feature of Boost Serialization that monitors if an object is serialized more than once. Boost automatically enables object tracking for all serialized classes, ensuring no unnecessary data duplications. Let's explore this a bit further:

```
#include <sstream>
#include <boost/archive/text_oarchive.hpp>
#include <boost/archive/text_iarchive.hpp>

struct demo
{
  int number;
  template<class Archive>
  void serialize(Archive & ar, const unsigned int
version)
```

```
   {
       ar & number;
   }
};
```

Here, if class demo is serialized multiple times in the same archive, Boost will only save the first instance fully, while the subsequent instances are merely references to the first.

7.2. Polymorphic Archives

Boost Serialization also offers 'polymorphic archives', throwing a lifeline to those programming scenarios that require dynamic type safety. If a base object's reference or pointer is serialized and a derived object is retrieved, the serialized form of the object is required. Polymorphic archives ensure type information is embedded in the serialized data.

Consider the following code snippet:

```
#include <boost/archive/polymorphic_iarchive.hpp>
#include <boost/archive/polymorphic_oarchive.hpp>

struct base
{
   virtual ~base() {}
   virtual void
serialize(boost::archive::polymorphic_oarchive & ar,
unsigned version) = 0;
   virtual void
serialize(boost::archive::polymorphic_iarchive & ar,
unsigned version) = 0;
};
BOOST_SERIALIZATION_ASSUME_ABSTRACT(base)
```

Here, we use two different function signatures for input and output serialization. Boost requires polymorphic archives to be non-intrusive, so any virtual function used is also declared within the relevant class.

7.3. Handling pointers and classes without default constructors

Boost Serialization can brilliantly handle pointers and classes without default constructors. Let's look at a code example:

```cpp
class boost_demo
{
private:
  friend class boost::serialization::access;
  template<class Archive>
  void serialize(Archive & ar, const unsigned int version)
  {
      ar & data;
  }
  int *data;
public:
  boost_demo(int value) : data(new int(value)) {}
  ~boost_demo() { delete data; }
};
```

Here we have a class with no default constructor, boost_demo, and the destructor releases heap memory. Even under complex conditions like these, it can be serialized normally with Boost Serialization.

7.4. Making Use of Versioning

Versioning is a gorgeous feature of Boost Serialization. It fusses around the changes made to a class over different versions of a library, requiring each version of the serialized class to be readable and maximally compatible.

Consider this illustration:

```
struct boost_version
{
  int x;
  template<class Archive>
  void save(Archive & ar, const unsigned int version)
const
  {
      ar & x;
      if(version > 0) ar & y;
  }
  template<class Archive>
  void load(Archive & ar, const unsigned int version)
  {
      ar & x;
      if(version > 0) ar & y;
  }
  BOOST_SERIALIZATION_SPLIT_MEMBER()
};
BOOST_CLASS_VERSION(boost_version, 1)
```

Here, we see the BOOST_CLASS_VERSION macro which signifies the current version of the class boost_version.

7.5. Enhancing Binary Archives

Binary serialization can be a boon in saving disk space and boosting faster data access. In Boost Serialization, binary archives can be used to serialize data into a binary format.

Below is an illustrative snippet:

```
#include <fstream>
#include <boost/archive/binary_oarchive.hpp>

int main()
{
    std::ofstream file("archive.binary");
    boost::archive::binary_oarchive oa(file);
    int x = 7;
    oa << x;
}
```

In this example, the integer 'x' is serialized into a binary format using `boost::archive::binary_oarchive`.

This concludes our exploration of the advanced features of Boost Serialization. By delving into this detailed exploration, we've laid a solid foundation to further strengthen your prowess in Boost Serialization. Remember, like any other technical skill, mastery in this domain comes with practice and patience. So, enjoy your journey through the intricate terrains of Boost Serialization!

Chapter 8. The Art of Debugging in Boost Serialization

Debugging - an indispensable tool in the tool chest of any programmer. A particular challenge presents itself when dealing with complex libraries that manipulate underlying data structures - libraries like Boost Serialization. This text will aid in identifying, diagnosing, and addressing issues that might arise in using Boost Serialization through comprehensive illustrations, practical techniques, and focused guidance.

8.1. UNDERSTANDING THE ERRORS IN BOOST SERIALIZATION

Understanding an error and the context in which it's occurring is the first step in effective debugging. While attempting to serialize or deserialize objects with Boost Serialization, some of the most common types of errors include compilation errors, runtime errors, incorrect results, and asserts.

Compilation errors are the easiest to spot as the compiler will halt and point you to them directly. Runtime errors, incorrect results, and asserts, however, occur after the code has compiled and the program is running. They can be a little more elusive and require a certain knack to debug.

For example, if there's an error in the serialization or deserialization of an object, you might not realize it until much later when the serialized data produces incorrect results or causes an assert while being used.

First step - ensure that you're logging sufficient information in a format that's easy for both human readers and automated tools to parse. Boost Serialization has its logging facilities which can be utilized to understand the source of errors better.

8.2. UTILIZING BOOST SERIALIZATION'S DEBUGGING TOOLS

Boost Serialization provides several macros and tools to assist in debugging, such as:

- BOOST_CLASS_EXPORT: This macro helps in automatically registering classes for serialization, reducing the chance of missing to manually register a class that you intend to serialize.

You can further increase verbosity by using the BOOST_CLASS_TRACKING macro, which can help you inspect the stages of serialization of individual objects.

8.3. BREAKPOINTS AND STEPPING THROUGH THE CODE

Another traditional but crucial technique is setting breakpoints and stepping through the code. By using a debugger tool, you can examine the state of your program at particular points (breakpoints) or step through sections of the code line by line.

Understanding the Boost Serialization process and the associated code flow is crucial here. Knowledge of the primary components - such as Archive classes, Stream classes etc., their role in serialization, and how they interact is essential to effectively step through the code and identify any issues.

8.4. INSPECTING THE SERIALISED DATA

Inspecting the serialized data directly can provide insights into any issues occurring during serialization or deserialization. If you're using text archives for your serialization, you can easily open the serialized file in a text editor and inspect it line by line.

Even if you're using binary archives, you can still inspect the serialized data. However, it would require more effort as it involves converting raw data into a readable form.

8.5. CONCLUSION

Mastering the art of debugging in Boost Serialization can indeed be a challenge but is an essential ability to acquire. It forms the cornerstone for identifying and resolving issues related to complex data persistency quickly. Armed with these practical tools and techniques, you will undoubtedly be better prepared to tackle any challenges that head your way with Boost Serialization in C++.

Remember: When debugging Boost.Serialization, understanding the context, utilising the available tools judiciously, setting breakpoints in the correct spots, and inspecting serialized data diligently will serve you well in your debugging journey. You're now set to explore a realm rich with features, and practical experience that stems from dealing hands-on is the best teacher.

Though the intricacies sometimes feel daunting, the sense of accomplishment when you master them is profound. To have wrestled with complexity and emerged victorious - that marks you as a true software craftsman. Now, go forth and code!

Chapter 9. Critical Evaluation: Boost Serialization vs Other Persistence Tools

Boost Serialization is a powerful, flexible tool that offers a high level of functionality and customizability. However, before unraveling its complexities and diving deep into its functionalities, let's take a moment to analyze and compare it to other popular persistence tools available in the realm of C++.

The four primary frameworks that are often pitted against Boost Serialization are the Standard Template Library (STL), Protocol Buffers, FlatBuffers, and the Cereal Library. The comparison will not only be limited to features, but we will also consider performance, ease of use, active community, stability, and cross-platform compatibility among others.

9.1. STL

Starting with STL, it's the heart of most C++ applications. The standard Containers, Algorithms, and Iterators provided by the STL aid in the development of robust, maintainable, and reusable software components. STL, however, does not inherently provide any built-in serialization support. This means that for every custom data structure, users must manually implement the serialization and deserialization functionality. As one can imagine, this is not only a time-consuming process, but it also introduces potential for errors and discrepancies.

However, with STL's excellent compatibility with Boost Serialization, there is a silver lining. It can be relatively straightforward to implement serialization for STL containers with Boost.

9.2. Protocol Buffers

Moving onto Google's Protocol Buffers (protobuf), a language-neutral, platform-neutral, and extensible method for serializing structured data. It's beneficial when building distributed applications, storing large amounts of data, and communication between services. Protocol Buffers requires the user to define how you want your data to be structured once, and then it auto-generates source code to write/read the data to/from a variety of data streams.

On the brighter side, protobuf is faster than Boost in some scenarios, especially in network communication. On the other hand, protobuf incurs extra overhead of maintaining a separate schema (.proto files), and the serialized data is not human-readable. It also tends to be more complex when dealing with nested and recursive data structures compared to Boost Serialization.

9.3. FlatBuffers

FlatBuffers, also from Google, offers an efficient cross-platform serialization library. It allows you to read serialized data without unpacking or parsing it entirely; it may be accessed directly. An advantage of using FlatBuffers is its incredibly high performance and efficient memory usage. It shines in applications where performance is critical, like in games and real-time systems.

However, just like Protocol Buffers, it also requires maintenance of separate schema (.fbs files), and it has a learning curve associated with it, especially for novice programmers. Unlike Boost, FlatBuffers lacks backward and forward compatibility and does not support XML or text archives out of the box.

9.4. Cereal

Lastly, Cereal is a header-only C++11 serialization library which is fast, light-weight, and easy to use. It provides comprehensive support for a broad range of standard library types and can serialize types from external libraries such as Boost. However, its performance does not generally match Protobuf or FlatBuffers.

Cereal does provide a cleaner syntax and less boilerplate code as it utilizes C++11 features, but it lacks backward compatibility and versioning. Also, despite a simpler API, it might sometimes be too simplistic and lack the flexibility and control provided by Boost Serialization.

9.5. Boost Serialization

Now, let's return to Boost Serialization. It brings great flexibility, including XML and text archive support, excellent backward and forward compatibility, and automatic serialization for STL and Boost containers, eliminating a significant amount of boilerplate code.

Boost Serialization caters to both simple and complex scenarios with relative ease. It handles recursive and nested data structures effortlessly, and the serialized data can be human-readable with XML and text archives.

On the flip side, Boost Serialization finds its weaknesses in large datasets, network communication, and real-time systems, where performance can be critical. Protobuf and FlatBuffers outperform Boost in these scenarios. However, Boost makes up for it by providing more features, flexibility, and control over the serialization process.

While Boost Serialization may not always be the fastest, it maintains a reasonable balance between features, performance, and control. Its rich flexibility makes it suitable for a broad range of situations, from smaller projects with simple requirements to larger projects with complex, change-prone data structures.

Different tools serve different purposes, and the choice ultimately boils down to the specific use case and requirements. The goal should always be selecting a tool that simplifies the process of serialization, and Boost Serialization proves to be a competent and flexible choice in numerous scenarios.

In the end, our journey revolves around Boost Serialization because it's a native part of the C ecosystem (Boost library), making it more straightforward to use and integrate into C projects. It allows transparent, yet powerful control of the serialization process without needing to maintain any external schemas or code generators, thus easing development.

Chapter 10. Performance Tuning and Efficiency Optimization in Boost Serialization

Among the key facets of Boost Serialization is the breadth of control it provides in fine-tuning performance and optimizing efficiency. This mastery is achievable via a robust analytical understanding of the library's core techniques and structures, while specifically targeting potential bottlenecks in the serialization process.

10.1. Understanding the Basics

The essence of Boost Serialization's performance tuning lies in a deep understanding of its concepts and functioning. Serialization in Boost primarily comprises two operations - saving (also called packing or exporting) and loading (unpacking or importing).

Saving involves persisting the state of data structures in a binary or text archive by recursively iterating through them. The archive is a stream into which the data structure is serialized, and it contains the serialized data once the saving operation is completed. For every type T that is serialized, Boost Serialization requires a `void serialize(Archive& ar, T& object, const unsigned version)` free-function or member-function.

Loading is the reverse operation where a data structure is reconstructed from the serialized data present in the archive. The library guarantees that data structures serialized and then deserialized (i.e., saved and then loaded) will have an identical state, irrespective of the configuration of either the saving environment or the loading environment.

10.2. Profiling Serialization

Before delving into the approaches to make your serialization more efficient, it's imperative to understand where it needs refining, which you can achieve through profiling. You can use member timers for each serialize function and supplement a profiler tool to understand which parts of your serialization are taking the most time. This way, you can find the methods/objects that are in dire need of optimization.

10.3. Selective Serialization

Selective Serialization allows you to choose the data structure members to be serialized, reducing the size of the serialized output and bringing about a substantial reduction in both time and space complexity. This is achieved by overriding the template specialization technique to provide a detailed implementation of saving and loading methods for the objects in question.

Example code of selective serialization:

```
template <typename Archive>
void serialize(Archive & ar, MyType& obj, const unsigned
int version)
{
    if(Archive::is_saving::value)
    {
        ar & obj.a;
    }
    else
    {
        ar & obj.a & obj.b & obj.c;
    }
}
```

10.4. Using Non-Default Constructors

Instead of using the default constructor and then loading the values, we can optimize the loading process and the construction with a non-default constructor that includes the archive as an argument. But do know that non-intrusive serialization doesn't support non-default constructor variants.

Example of this implementation:

```
template<typename Archive>
Child(Archive& ar)
{
    ar >> *this;
}
```

10.5. Adjusting Archive Buffer Size

Boost serialization uses file streams for reading or writing to files, be it text or binary. The I/O operations, particularly file operations, can be a bottleneck if not properly managed. By using the rdbuf function of file stream, you can adjust the buffer size allocated for reading/writing based on your specific needs, thus minimizing the need for file write/read operations, which are expensive compared to memory operations.

10.6. Data Marshaling

Boost Serialization library doesn't inherently support marshaling, but you can pack the serialized data into a string using `boost::iostreams::back_insert_device` mechanism and then transmit this string to the user for unmarshaling.

10.7. Optimizing for Large Collections

When dealing with large collections, split serialization for saving and loading can bring significant enhancements in terms of performance. This is because, for large collections, the library has to keep track of serialized items and perform lookups to determine if a particular item has been serialized already. Through split serialization, we can bypass object tracking by creating separate save and load functions.

A snippet of split member serialization is as follows:

```cpp
template<class Archive>
void save(Archive & ar, const unsigned int version)
const
{
    ar & boost::serialization::base_object<Base>(*this);
    ar & someData;
}

template<class Archive>
void load(Archive & ar, const unsigned int version)
{
    ar & boost::serialization::base_object<Base>(*this);
    ar & someData;
}

BOOST_SERIALIZATION_SPLIT_MEMBER()
```

Implementing these optimization techniques in Boost Serialization will surely pave the way to faster and more efficient serialization processes. As you continue to work further with Boost Serialization, you will also find some other techniques on your own that might help improve efficiency and performance. Remember, every application is unique in its requirements, so there's no one-size-fits-all answer to how you can optimize your serialization. The key lies in understanding your application's specific needs and the expertise gained from your experiences. Happy Coding!

Chapter 11. Future Perspectives: Trends and Developments in Boost Serialization

As we cast our gaze into the future, the vivid impression of Boost Serialization's potential and future advancements solidify. The trends and developments bring forth a promising landscape for C++ developers, which can revolutionize data persistence techniques. This chapter will delve into the significance of Boost Serialization's role in future applications and analyze the emerging trends to prepare developers for tomorrow.

11.1. The Evolution of Boost Serialization

Boost Serialization began as a humble solution for basic data persistence needs. Over time, it has evolved into a comprehensive and efficient system for preserving and restoring data. The incremental improvements in syntax, performance, and breadth of compatibility with different data types have distinguished it as a cornerstone of C++ project development. The continuous growth and enhancement of Boost Serialization is a trend expected to persist into the foreseeable future.

The focus of future developments is on enhancing its user-friendliness, efficiency, flexibility, and expanding its capacity to handle more complex data structures. Asynchrony is another promising arena where Boost can expand, allowing for non-blocking operations, which will represent a significant leap in performance.

Internetwork operability is another frontier open for development. Boost Serialization's current rendition focuses on single-system operations. An expansion to permit efficient serialization across networked systems would transform C++ software development and expand its sphere of influence radically.

11.2. Powering Ahead with Infrastructure Improvements

Continual infrastructure improvements are crucial as they increase the quality of software development projects. As Better Resource Acquisition Is Initialization (RAII) principles become a universal standard, you can expect integration with smart pointers to improve. Moreover, higher emphasis is being placed on exception safety and multithread safety, crucial for writing reliable, large-scale applications.

The dawn of the era of cloud computing and distributed systems necessitates serialization libraries to be adaptable and efficient on a larger scale. Boost Serialization will need to further optimize its algorithms, data structures, and systems to compete effectively.

11.3. Embrace the Dominance of Big Data

Big Data is increasingly becoming central to software development. Serialization plays a significant role in transferring data between different systems and processes. To manage data efficiently, improvements must be made in compression techniques. As of now, data size is an apparent limitation of Boost Serialization, which future developments must address.

Expect to see more significant improvements in handling larger volumes of data with lesser redundancy. Technologies such as data chunking or segmentation and differential serialization, which only serializes the differences between versions of an object, might come to the fore.

11.4. Compatibility with Other Libraries

Intersectionality between different libraries can maximize a developer's efficiency by leveraging the benefits of each. Boost Serialization could move towards being more synergistic with other Boost libraries, and even libraries outside the Boost ecosystem.

This would transform the process of software development, making it more seamless, efficient, and programmer-friendly. In practical terms, this might mean improvements like out-of-the-box compatibility with more container and data types, and more effective serialization for objects of the Boost MultiArray or Boost Graph Library.

11.5. Streamlined Error Handling

Looking forward, error handling in Boost Serialization could become more intuitive and straightforward. The addition of robust debugging and error logging features, for example, has the potential to revolutionize error management. Programmers could see improvements such as reduced time spent hunting for mysterious serialization errors.

From another perspective, providing detailed diagnostic messages for serialization failures directly linked to the source, type, and location of the error in a user-friendly way would be a welcome change for the developer community.

11.6. Final Thoughts on Future Perspectives

Trends and advancements in Boost Serialization hold immense possibilities. It's vital for developers to stay informed about such developments. It's clear that the landscape of Boost Serialization is multifold, improving efficiency, enhancing compatibility, handling Big Data effectively, and streamlining error management. Developers must leverage these improvements to elevate their codebases. The journey to the future is marked by the footprints of these trends, promising an exhilarating journey onward in software development with Boost Serialization. Rest assured, the exploration and mastery of these upcoming trends will equip you to be a part of this exciting voyage. Embrace the challenges and remember, every line of code is a step towards the future.

www.ingramcontent.com/pod-product-compliance
Lightning Source LLC
LaVergne TN
LVHW010041070326
832903LV00071B/4614